· PLAIN GIRL ·

Also by Arthur Miller

Plays
After the Fall
All My Sons
The American Clock
The Archbishop's Ceiling
Broken Glass
The Creation of the World, and Other Business
The Crucible
Danger: Memory!
Death of a Salesman
An Enemy of the People (adapted from Ibsen)
The Golden Years
Incident at Vichy
The Last Yankee
The Man Who Had All the Luck
A Memory of Two Mondays
The Price
The Ride Down Mount Morgan
Two-Way Mirror
Up From Paradise
A View from the Bridge

Screenplays
Everybody Wins
The Misfits
Playing for Time

Prose fiction
Focus
I Don't Need You Any More
Jane's Blanket (for children)

Non-fiction
The Theatre Essays of Arthur Miller
'Salesman' in Beijing

With Inge Morath
Chinese Encounters
In Russia
In the Country

Autobiography
Timebends

ARTHUR MILLER

· PLAIN GIRL ·

A life

Methuen

Published by Methuen 2000

1 3 5 7 9 10 8 6 4 2

First published in the United States by Peter Blum Books
under the title *Homely Girl: A Life*
First published in Great Britain in 1995 by Methuen
and reissued in 1996 by Minerva

This paperback published in 2000 by Methuen Publishing Ltd
215 Vauxhall Bridge Rd, London SW1V 1EJ

Methuen Publishing Limited Reg. No. 3543167

A CIP catalogue record for this book
is available from the British Library

ISBN 0 413 74670 4

Typeset by Deltatype Ltd, Birkenhead, Merseyside
Printed and bound in Great Britain by
Cox & Wyman Ltd, Reading, Berkshire

· PLAIN GIRL ·

· I ·

Janice awoke feeling cold that Monday morning, which was odd – a wind seemed to blow on her as she surfaced up from a deep sleep, already recalling that it was June and that yesterday had been warm in Central Park. And opening her eyes as usual toward him she saw how strangely blanched his face was. Although what she called his sleeping smile was still there, and the usual suggestion of happiness at the curled corners of his mouth. But he seemed heavier on the mattress and she knew immediately and with dread raised her hand and touched his cheek, the end of the long story. Her first thought, like an appeal against a mistake, 'But he is only sixty-eight!'

Fright but no tears, not outside. Just the thump on the back of her neck. Life had a fist.

'Ah!' she pitied aloud and bringing palms together touched fingers to her lips. 'Ah!' She bent to him, her silky hair touching his face. But he wasn't there. 'Ah, Charles!' A little anger soon dispersed by reason. And wonder.

The wonder remained. That after all her life had amounted to a little something, had given her this man, this man who had never seen her. He was awesome now, lying there.

Oh, if one more time she could have spoken with him, asked or told him . . . what? The thing in her heart, the wonder. That he had loved her and had never seen her in the fourteen years of their life together. Always, despite everything, something in her trying to move itself into his line of vision as though with one split-second glimpse of her his fluttering eyes would wake from their eternal sleep.

Now what do I do? Oh, Charles dear, what do I do with the rest of it?

Something was not finished. But I suppose, she said to herself, nothing ever is except in movies when the lights come on, leaving you squinting on the sidewalk.

Once more she moved to touch him, but already he was not there, not hers, not anything, and she withdrew her hand and sat there with one leg overhanging the mattress.

She had hated her face as a girl but knew she had
style and at least once a day settled for that and
her very good compact body and a terrific long
neck. And yes, her irony. She was and wanted to
be a snob. She knew how to slip a slight, witty
rotation into her hips when she walked, although
she had no illusions that it made up for a pulled
look to her cheeks, as if alum had tightened her
skin, and an elongated upper lip. A little like
Disraeli, she thought once, coming on his picture
in a high-school text. And a too-high forehead
(she refused to overlook anything negative). She
wondered if she'd been drawn out of the womb
and lengthened, or her mother startled by a
giraffe. At parties she had many a time noticed
how men coming up behind her were caught
surprised when she turned to face them. But she
had learned to shake out the straight silky light
brown hair and flick the ironic defensive grin,
silent pardon for their inevitable fade. She had a
tonic charm and it was almost – although not
quite, of course – enough, not since childhood
and her mother holding up a Cosmopolitan Ivory
ad to her face and so warmly and lovingly
exclaiming, 'Now that's beauty!' as though by
staring at it hard enough she could be made to
look like one of those girls. She felt blamed then.

Still, at fifteen she believed that between her ankles and her breasts she was as luscious as Betty Grable, or almost. And she had a soft provocative lisp that men seemed to like who had an interest in mouths. At sixteen Aunt Ida, visiting from Egypt, had said, 'You've got an Egyptian look, Egyptian women are hot.' Recalling that oddity would make her laugh and raised her spirits even into her sixties after Charles had died.

A number of memories involved lying in bed on a Sunday morning, listening thankfully to muffled New York outside. 'I was just thinking – apropos of nothing,' she whispered into Charles's ear one time, 'that for at least a year after Sam and I had separated I was terribly embarrassed to say we had. And even after you and I married, whenever I had to refer to "my first husband" it curdled something inside me. Like a disgrace or a defeat. What a simple-minded generation we were!'

Sam was beneath her in some indefinite class sense, but that was part of his attraction in the thirties when to have been born to money was shameful, a guarantee of futility. People her age, early twenties then, wanted to signify by doing good, attended emergency meetings a couple of times a week in downtown lofts or sympathisers'

West End Avenue living rooms to raise money for organising the new National Maritime Union or ambulances for the Spanish Republicans, and they were moved to genuine outrage at Fascism, which was somehow a parents' system and the rape of the mind; the Socialist hope was for the young, for her, and no parent could help fearing its subversive beauty. Anyway, hers were hopelessly silly people, Jews putting on the dog with a new absurd name endowed on them by the Immigration Inspectors back in the other century because Great-Grandpa's original Russian one was unpronounceable by their Irish tongues. So they were Sessions.

But Sam was Fink, which she rather relished as a taunt to her father, long a widower and very ill now although still being consulted on the phone as an authority on utilities by the time of her marriage, dying as he read that Hitler had walked into Vienna. 'But he won't last,' he whispered scoffingly across the cancer in his throat. 'The Germans are too intelligent for this idiot.' Of course by now she knew better, knew a world was ending and would not be surprised to see American Storm Troopers with chin-straps on Broadway one evening. It was already scary to go walking around in Yorkville on the Upper East

Side where the Germans were rallying on the street corners to bait Jews and praise Hitler on summertime Saturday nights. She was not particularly Semitic-looking, but she feared the fear of the prey as she passed thick-necked men on 86th Street.

A stylish man, her father, with a long noble head and an outmoded mind, or so she thought of him in the flush of her new-found revolutionary independence. Stroking his cold hand in the gloom of the West End Avenue apartment she thanked her luck or rather her own perceptive intelligence, for having helped turn her away from all this heavy European silverware, the overstuffed chairs and the immense expanse of Oriental carpet, the sheer doomed weight of their possessions and the laughable confidence it had once expressed. If not beautiful she was at least strong, free of Papa's powerful illusions. But now that he was weak and his eyes were closed most of the time she could let herself admit that she shared his arrogant style, caring a lot and pretending not to, unlike her mother who'd screamingly pretended to care and hadn't at all. But of course Papa accepted the injustice in the world as natural, like trees, while for her it was often an unbearable waste. An outwardly conventional man, he was quickly bored by predictable people and had linked her to him by his secret mockery of uniformity which had fuelled her rebellion against her mother. A day before he died he smiled at her and said, 'Don't worry, Janice, you're pretty enough, you'll be okay, you've got the guts.' If only okay could ever be enough.

The Rabbi's brief ceremony must have been developed for these bankrupt times; people were scanting even these rote funerary farewells to get back to their gnawing make-a-living worries. Following the prayer the funeral chapel man, looking like H. L. Mencken with hair parted in the middle, shot his starched cuffs and picked up the small cardboard box of ashes, handing it to her fat brother Herman who in his surprise looked at it like a ticking explosive. Then they went out into the hot sunlit street and walked downtown together. Herman's butterball wife Edna kept falling behind to look into an occasional shoe store window, one of the few still occupied in whole blocks of vacancies along Broadway. Half New York seemed to be for rent, with permanent signs bolted to nearly every apartment house announcing vacancies. Herman flopped his feet down like a seal as he walked, sucking for breath. 'Look at it, the whole block,' he said with a wave of his hand.

'Real estate doesn't interest me right now,' she said.

'Oh, it doesn't? Maybe eating does, cause this is where he put a lot of your money, baby.' They sat at a darkened Irish bar on 84th Street facing Broadway with an electric fan blowing into their faces. 'Did you hear? Roosevelt's supposed to have syph.'

'I'm trying to drink this, please.' Defying ritual and capitalist superstition she wore a beige skirt and a shiny white silk blouse and high-heeled tan shoes. Sam had to be in Syracuse to bid on an important library being auctioned. 'You must be the last Republican Jew in New York,' she said to her brother.

Herman wheezed, absently moving the little box around on the bar like the final beleaguered piece in a lost chess game, a futile three inches in one direction and then in the other. He sipped his beer and talked about Hitler, the remorseless heat that summer, and real estate.

'These refugees are coming over and buying up Amsterdam Avenue.'

'So what difference does that make?'

'Well, they're supposed to be so down-trodden.'

'You want them more downtrodden? Don't you understand anything? Now that Franco's won Hitler's going to attack Russia, there's going to be a tremendous war. And all you can think of is real estate.'

'So what if he attacks Russia?'

'Oh God, I'm going home.' Disgust flowed up her back and glancing at the little box she drank her second Martini fast; how really weird, a whole man fitting into a four-by-six-inch carton hardly big enough for a few muffins.

'If you'd throw some of your share in with mine we could pick up buildings for next to nothing. This Depression won't last forever and we could clean up some day.'

'You really know how to pick a time to talk about business.' He had all Papa's greed but with a baby face and none of his charm. Slipping off her stool, smiling angrily, she gave him a moni-tory bop on the head with her purse, kissed round Edna's plump cheek, and with heels clacking walked into the street, Herman behind her defending his right to be interested in real estate.

She was halfway home in the taxi when she

recalled that at some point he had bequeathed the ashes to her. Had he remembered to take them from the bar? She called him. Scandalised, he piped, 'You mean you lost them?' She hung up, cutting him off, scared. She had left Papa on the bar. She went weak in the thighs with some superstitious fear that surprised her. All her atheistic dismissal of religion collapsed and she had to reason it back. After all, she thought, what is the body? Only the *idea* of a person matters, and Papa's in my heart. Running a bath and approaching transcendence again in the remnants of her yellow Martini haze, she glimpsed her unchangeable face in the steamy mirror and the body mattered again. Yet at the same time it didn't. She tried to recall a classical philosopher who might have reconciled the two truths, but tired of the effort. Then realising she had bathed only a few hours earlier she shut off the tap and began to dress again.

She found she was hurrying and knew she had to get the ashes back, she had done an awful thing leaving them there, something like sin. For a moment her father lived again, reprimanding her with a sad look. But at the same time it was somehow humorous, in a vaguely tasteless way.

The bartender, a thin, long-armed man,

recalled no such box. He asked if there was anything valuable in it and she said, 'Well, no.' Then the guilt butted her like a goat. 'My father. His ashes.'

'Holy Jesus!' The man's eyes widened at this omen of bad luck. His flaring emotion startled her into weeping. It was the first time and she felt grateful to him, and also ashamed that he might feel more about Papa than she did. He touched her back with his hand and guided her to the dismal Ladies Room in the rear but looking around she found nothing. The bartender was odourless, like Vaseline, and for a split instant she wondered if this was all a dream. She stared down at the toilet. Oh God, what if someone sprinkled Papa down there! Returning to the bar she touched the man's thick tattooed forearm. 'It doesn't matter,' she reassured him. He insisted on giving her a drink and she had a Martini, and they talked about different kinds of death, sudden and drawn-out, the deaths of the very young and the old. Her eyes were red-rimmed. Two gas company workers at the bar listened in their brutal solemnity from a respectful distance. It had always been more relaxing to be among strange men than with women she didn't know. The bartender came around the bar to see her to the door and before she could think she had kissed him on the cheek. 'Thank you,' she said. Sam had never really pursued her, she thought now, she had more or less granted herself. She walked down Broadway angering with regret at their marriage and by the time she reached the corner loved, or at least pitied him again.

And so Papa was gone. After a few blocks she felt relieved as she sensed the gift of mourning in her, that illusion of connection with the past; but how strange that the emotion should have been given to her by a probably right-wing Catholic Irishman who most likely supported Franco and couldn't stand Jews. Everything was feeling, nothing was clear. Somehow, this sudden, unexpected collision with the barman's authentic feeling cast a light – she saw that she really must stop waiting to become someone else, she was Janice forever. What an exciting idea! If she could follow it maybe it would lead her to solid ground. It was like the Depression itself – everybody kept waiting for it to lift and forgot how to live in the meantime, but supposing it went on forever? She must start living! And Sam had to stop thinking so exclusively about Fascism and organising unions and the rest of the endlessly repetitious radical agenda . . . . But she mustn't think that way, she guiltily corrected herself.

She smiled, reminded of her newly orphaned liberation. In a few minutes, walking down Broadway, she saw something amusing in so formal and fastidious a man as Dave Sessions being left in a box on a bar – she could see him trapped in there, tiny, outraged and red-faced, banging on the lid to be let out. A strange thought struck her – that the body was more of an abstraction than the soul, which never disappeared.

Sam Fink had a warming smile, an arched bony nose which, as he said, he had been years learning to love. He was just about Janice's five feet seven, and standing face to face with him sometimes brought to mind her mother's nasty, repeated warning, 'Never marry a handsome man.' Which Janice had taken as a barely disguised jab not only at beautiful Papa's vanity but at her own looks. But unhandsome Sam had a different beauty, a certain reverent and selfless social vision, and an absolute devotion to her. Sam and his Communist commitment brought her closer to the future and away from her nemesis, triviality, the bourgeois obsession with things.

But it was painful to look at pictures in museums with him at her side – she had majored in art history at Hunter – and to hear nothing about Picasso but his conversion to the Party or the secret anti-monarchical codes buried in Titian's paintings or the class-struggle metaphor in Rembrandt. 'They are not necessarily conscious of it, of course, but the great ones were always in a struggle with the ruling class.'

'But darling, all that has nothing to do with painting.'

And spoken with a teacher's gently superior grin toward a child – and incipient violence in his eyes, 'Except that it has everything to do with painting; their convictions were what raised them above the others, the "painters". You have to learn this, Janice, conviction matters.'

Browbeaten by his self-denying faith she was somehow reassured about herself. Tucking her arm under his as they walked she supposed most people married not out of overwhelming love but to find justification in one another, and why not? Glancing at his powerful nose and neat, nearly bald head she felt elevated by his moral nature and safe in his militancy. But it was not always possible to banish the vision of an empty space surrounding them, a lightless gloom into

which something horrible could suddenly step one day.

It was his amazing knowledge of books that helped quiet her doubts. What class Sam had came from the immense number of books he had prideful knowledge of, the dates of their authors and where in England or America they had lived, they being mostly American and British writers his customers were interested in collecting. He was one of the few book dealers who read what he was selling, could pick out of the air the names of authorities on a couple of hundred subjects from chess to China, as he snappily put it to his awed customers — who forgave his arrogance in view of his encyclopaedic mind. He also knew the locations of dozens of old mansions all over New York State, Connecticut, Massachusetts and New Jersey where expiring old families still had sizeable libraries to get rid of on the death of some final aunt, uncle or inheriting retainer. A couple of times a month he would drive into the country in his green stiff-sprung Nash for a day or two and return with trunk and back seat packed with sets of Dickens, Thackeray, Melville, Hawthorne, Shakespeare; armfuls of mouse-nibbled miscellany; an 1868 *Survey of Literature of the Womb*; a 1905 *Manual of Chinese*

Enamelware; *Lasting Irish Melodies* of 1884; *Annals of Ophthalmology* or *Laryngial Surgery*; and Janice would sit with him on the floor of their dark East 32nd Street living room, she imagining the silent sealed-up life of families in some upper Monroe County household from whose privacy these books had been ripped, books that must once have brought news of the great world out and beyond their lilac doorways. Meanwhile he hungrily entered in a school notebook the publication dates of each volume, their condition and all the pertinent information his customers would require. His plain love for his books and his work stirred her love for him. He even loved the books themselves and would lift choice passages from Trollope especially, or Henry James or Virginia Woolf, or Communist Louis Aragon and the young Richard Wright, reading to her with the proprietary self-congratulation of an author. He was snobbish like her, but unlike her, denied it. Sitting cross-legged on the oriental carpet she thought he had the simple spiritual look of a cute monk, including the innocent round tonsure. And there was something monkish in his pretence of not noticing – when she leaned back resting on her elbows, one leg tucked under and her skirt midway up her thigh

— that she was asking to be taken there on the floor. Seeing him flush and shift to some explication of the day's news she despaired for herself. Still, with the so-called democracies unquestionably flirting with Fascism she could hardly ask him to set her greedy desire ahead of serious things.

Alone at least two evenings a week when he went to Party meetings, she walked across the dead East Side over to slummy 6th with its tenements under the El and dusty Irish bars and came home tired to listen to Benny Goodman records and smoked too many Chesterfields until she was tensed and angry at the walls. When Sam came home, heatedly explaining Stalin's latest utterances on how the Socialist future, bearing goodness at last, was moving as inexorably toward them as an ocean wave, she nearly drowned in her own ingratitude, and was only calmed by the vision of justice which he was guarding along with the nameless army of civilised comrades spread out across every country in the world.

On another Sunday morning in bed with Charles, forever trying to visualise herself, she said, 'I can never figure out what got me — it was about four years after being married — we'd usually come home from a French or Russian movie on Irving Place and go to bed, and that was that. This time I decided to make myself a Martini and then sat on the couch listening to records, you know like Benny Goodman's "Blue Moon" or the Billie Holiday things or Leadbetter, or maybe Woody Guthrie I think was coming on at that time, and after twenty minutes Sam came out of the bedroom in his pyjamas. He was really shy but he wasn't a coward and he stood there, poor man, with that tense grin, leaning on the bedroom door jamb like Humphrey Bogart, and he said, "Sleep-time."

'That's when it just fell out of my mouth. "Fuck the future," I said.'

Charles's eyelids fluttered and he laughed with her and pressed his hand on the inside of her thigh.

'He laughed, but blushing — you know, that I'd said that word. And he said, "What does that mean?"

' "Just fuck the future." ' She heard her own tinkling giggle and would always remember the free-falling feeling in her chest.

'It must have a meaning.'

'It means that there must be something happening now that is interesting and worth thinking about. And now means now.'

'Now always means now.' He grinned against apprehension.

'No, it mostly means pretty soon, or some day. But now it means tonight.'

Angered, Sam blushed deeper, redness staining his high forehead. She opened the dark oak cabinet and made another Martini and giggling at some secret joke got into bed and drank it to the bottom. Feeling left out he could only go on idealistically grinning, brave man, elbow on the pillow, trying hard to get a grasp on her spinning mind.

'Papa and I once lived in this Portuguese beachhouse for a month after Mama died, and I used to watch this peasant cook we had coming over the sand-dunes carrying fresh vegetables and a fish in a basket for me to inspect so she could cook it for us. She'd take forever trudging in the sand till she got to me, and then all it was was this fish, which was still damp from the ocean.'

'What about it?'

'Well, that's it – you wait and wait and watch it coming and it's a damp fish.' She had laughed and laughed, helplessly nearing hysteria, then brushed a dismissive kiss on Sam's wrist and fell into a separate sleep smiling with some uncertain air of victory.

Now she ran a finger lightly along Charles's nose. 'Did any of that mean anything to you – the Left?'

'I was studying music in the thirties.'

'How wonderful. Just studying music.'

'You make it all sound such a waste. Was it, you think?'

'I don't know yet. When I think of the writers we all thought were so important, and no one knows their names any more. I mean the militant people. That whole literature simply dribbled away. Gone.'

'It was a style, wasn't it? Most styles crack up and disappear.'

'What are you trying to tell me?' she asked, kissing his earlobe.

'You seem to have a need to mock yourself as you were then. I don't think you should. A lot of the past is always embarrassing – if you have any sensitivity.'

'Not for you, though.'

'Oh, I've had plenty of moments.'

'That you're ashamed of?'

He nodded. She felt she was blushing for him

and could not press him. She did not want his
nobility marred. Some day he might tell her. In
fact, she was aware of how really little she knew
of his life. 'Radicals think they want truth, but
what they really long for is high-minded characters to look up to.'

'Not only radicals, Janice. People have to
believe in goodness.' His eyelids fluttered faster
when he was excited and they did so now, like
birds' wings. 'They're disappointed most of the
time but in some part of his beliefs every person
is naïve. Even the most cynical. And memories of
one's naïvety are always painful. But so what?
Would you rather have had no beliefs at all?'

She buried her face in his flesh. His acceptance
of her, she thought, was like a tide.

One of the worst days she remembered was
when the stunning news exploded on the radio
that Stalin had made the non-aggression pact
with Hitler. Stalin had always been the bulwark
against the mind-hating Nazis as well as the
corrupted British and French upper-class snobs
secretly longing for Fascism in their own countries. The Pact rained down the threat of a new
Unreason on many a mind in the city, the world.

'How can it have happened?' she asked Sam.

They were on 8th Street, at a place called Barclay's where dinner was ninety cents rather than the sixty-five next door in the University Inn. The Village was stunned, probing Stalin's mind, struggling not to give up on the Soviets. For her, Stalin having so much as touched Hitler was like God having sex, eating food and farting. The Soviet had been the sublime opposite of West End Avenue, of carpets and silverware and the dry futility of life in the middle-class city.

Sam tapped the side of his nose with a wink and a canny grin, a sophistication meant to throw off his unease. 'Don't worry, Stalin knows what he's doing; and he's not helping Hitler, he'll never supply Germany.'

'But he is, isn't he?'

'He is not. He's just refusing to pull the French and British chestnuts out of the fire. He's been pleading with them for a pact against Hitler for five years now, and they've stalled, hoping Hitler would attack Russia. Well, he's turned the chess game around.'

She glanced about in the restaurant. Most of the diners were in their twenties, a few middle-aged. Frequently in the past the owner or a customer acquaintance would stop by to ask Sam's analysis of some political development:

people sought out his reassuring certainty. Lately no one was stopping by, and on their way out the owner weakly waved to them from a far corner. Nobody, she thought, knows what to think any more, and they don't think Sam knows either.

In that wearing and parched year-and-a-half interval, she had seen Sam Fink straining to justify the Pact to her and to their friends. And when it was no longer deniable that Russian wheat and oil were actually being shipped to a Germany that was invading France, something within her came to a halt and stood motionless behind her eyes, stunned. Trained to reason or think its way toward hope, her brain was sinking into cynicism and she finally stashed the whole business in the part of her being which she quite consciously labelled 'Denial Department', a space that was filling up.

Now the worst of it was her uncertainty about Sam's leadership. He was no more a cynic than she was, but what else to call this shutting of their eyes to facts? Old friends were dropping away, hopes in the Soviet foundering. 'Frankly, I am most of the time ashamed of saying I'm not anti-Soviet,' she dared to declare one night at dinner.

'The summer soldiers and sunshine patriots . . . ,' he started to mock.

'But Sam, they are helping Hitler.'

'The story hasn't ended yet.'

Twenty-five years on she would look back at this conversation, aware that she had known at the time that she was losing respect for Sam's leadership; and how odd that it should have come about because of a pact ten thousand miles away!

'But shouldn't we object? Shouldn't you?' she asked.

At that moment, instead of replying, his mouth formed a smile that to her seemed smug, and he shook his head pityingly. That was when it happened, the first cut of hatred for him, the first sense of insult. But of course she hung on, as one did in those times, and even pretended – not only to him but to herself – that she had absorbed another of his far-seeing lessons.

But part of it wasn't pretence; she knew that the best of Sam, his noble faithful loyalty, was being challenged, and she had to respect that if only because it was her own reassurance. She felt paralysed; how could she condemn what sprang from his goodness even as she knew it was supporting the wrong? It seemed to her she could love him madly if only he could admit that he was suffering in this dilemma, as she was sure he must be.

'I don't see any dilemma,' he said when she suggested there was one. 'Stalin is shaking the Devil's hand to save his country, and that is not wrong.'

They went to bed that night consciously cool, with the winds of the world crossing their faces. 'This must be a chapter for us,' she thought. 'Maybe now it will all change.'

If he could only admit how wounded he was! Oddly, she felt the need for healing him, for being loved then, for sex. But he seemed happily asleep. It must be a chapter. Closing her eyes she invited Cary Grant to lean over her and speak ironically as he undid his incredible bow-tie and slipped out of his clothes.

Still, maybe it was easier for a marriage to sustain two people lying than one. Until now only she had been the alien, now he must feel its artificiality too, she thought. But in his perfect denial he slept.

But the Village was relaxed again, a year and a half later, when Hitler finally broke the agreement and attacked Russia. All was well now that Fascism was the enemy again. The Russians were heroic and Janice felt a part of America once more, no longer so dreadfully ashamed of a partnership with Hitler.

Sam Fink presented himself at the 90 Church Street Navy Recruitment Office a week after Pearl Harbor, but with his name and his nose he was not Naval Officer material – the grin on the amused face of the blond examining Lieutenant Senior Grade was not lost on Sam, nor its irony in this anti-Fascist war – and so he went into the more democratic Army. The rebuff was embarrassing but not unexpected under capitalism, especially when for years now so many Jewish students had been having to go to Scottish and British medical schools, turned away by the *numerus clausus*, the quota system of American institutions. First Sam trained in Kentucky, then in the Officers' School in Fort Sill Oklahoma, while Janice waited in broiling hot wooden rooming houses off-base. The War might last eight or ten years, they were saying. But she must not complain, considering the bombing of London and the crucifixion of Yugoslavia. Desperately fighting loneliness she taught herself shorthand and typing just in case she never landed an editorial job at any of the offices and publishing houses to which she had begun to apply, now that they were losing men to the War.

But now she was twenty-eight and on bad nights her bored face – the face of a trim, small horse, she had decided – could bring her close to tears; then she would take a notebook and try to write her feelings out. 'It isn't that I feel positively unattractive – I know better. But that somehow I am being kept from anything miraculous happening to me, ever.'

With love for Sam dimmed, time lost its meaning, she no longer understood why she was doing anything. A saving miracle was becoming a less than strange idea. 'Somehow, when I look at myself, the miraculous seems to be more and more factually possible. Or is this hot room driving me crazy?' Hearing a line of tanks roaring past she would go out on the front stoop of their cottage and wave to the officers whose upper bodies like Centaurs stuck up out of the top portholes. When they were gone and the dust rained down sparkling in the rays of the moon she stood there wondering, 'Did we huddle together with one another, because we both felt unwanted?' This hateful affront, once it lodged in her brain, would send her more and more often to the bottle, and with a couple of drinks she would force the worst to her lips – 'He makes love like mailing a letter.' And then she would flush her note down the toilet.

Her rage, like everything else in this wartime, was on hold for the duration. She loved the *New Yorker*, especially Perelman and Thurber, and the slyly concealed arrogance of their humour. How fantastic to be able to display one's mind like this, one's personality! Suddenly it seemed to her that the worst of this War, and the Depression before it and the whole life she had led, was that it made you suppress everything but your goodness. Back inside the cottage she sat on the lumpy mattress and thought guiltily of poor Sam on bivouac, sleeping on the wet ground out there in the pinewoods. 'What an ungrateful bitch I am,' she said aloud. And falling back on to the damp pillow – 'That bastard Hitler!' – and swung out into sleep on her anger.

· II ·

When she recalled it all later her collision with Lionel Mayer would seem painfully ordinary, but at the time it sent her flying off the track of her old life. He and his wife Sylvia, a left-wing organiser for the Newspaper Guild, had been their friends for years by this time and he had been assigned as Press Officer in Sam's Division. That fall, ordered out on a five-day bivouac, Sam saw to it that Lionel would take her into Lovelock for dinner, giving up pretending that his wife was happy hanging around army camps. Janice was vaguely unnerved at the date; Lionel, ambitious to become a star actor after the War, was four years younger than she. With his thick black curly hair, powerful hands and a juicy sense of the outrageous he had always seemed to be inviting her curiosity about him; she had noticed how he nearly lost himself staring at women and it was easy to set him to performing for her with his impudent stories and jokes. He was interested in making love to her, she had come to believe, something hard to put together with his principled nature and shyness with his wife – until she thought of her own behaviour.

She had never been alone with him in a strange place, and he was a different man over dinner, holding her hand on the table, all but offering himself in his charged gaze. Calculating the risk, she thought it seemed low; he would clearly not want the undoing of his marriage any more than she wanted it for hers.

'You have grey eyes,' he said with a certain hunger which she found absurd and necessary.

'Two of them, yes.'

He burst out laughing, relieved that he would not have to continue the ploy. Walking back to the bus stop from the restaurant they saw the Rice Hotel sign overhead and both looked at each other and grinned, and her insides caved in like sand. If she were recognised going up the broad mahogany stairway with him then so be it; she numbly resolved not to stop the force that was carrying her forward and out of a dead life. Lionel descended on her like an ocean wave, tumbling her, invading her, pounding her past to bits. She had forgotten what stings of pleasure lay asleep in her groin, what lifts of feeling could swamp her brain. In the cottage afterwards, sliding back down to the bottom of her pit, she studied her sated face in the bathroom mirror and saw how slyly feminine she really was, how sombre and untruthful, and she happily winked. It flickered across her mind that she felt free once more, like when her father had died.

Kissing Sam goodbye the night he sailed for England, she thought he had never looked this handsome in his uniform and his shoulder bars and his fine double-breasted trench coat. But with the holy cause so nobly glowing in his face, his eyes, his manly grin, she mournfully knew she could not go on with him for life; even at his best it would not be enough. She was a real stinker, a total fraud. He insisted she stay behind in the apartment and not accompany him to the ship. A novel gravity in his look now; 'I know I'm not right for you, but . . .'

Guilt smashed her in the face; 'Oh but you are, you are!' What a thing to say when he might be going to his death!

'Well, maybe we'll figure it out when I come back.'

'Oh my darling. . . .' She clutched him closer

than she had ever wanted to before and he kissed her hard on the mouth in a way he'd never done.

It was still difficult for him to speak even though it might be their last moment together. 'I don't want you to think I don't know what's been happening.' He glanced at a wall to escape her eyes. 'I just haven't taken us seriously enough – I mean in a certain sense, and I regret it. . . .'

'I understand.'

'Maybe not altogether.' He looked straight at her now with his valorous warm smile. 'I guess I've thought of you as a partner in the Revolution, or something like that. And I've left out everything else, or almost everything. Because my one obsession has been Fascism, it's taken up all my thinking.' No, dear, it's sexual fear that's done that. 'But America is on the line now, not just people like me, and Hitler is finished. So if I do come back I want to start over as a couple. I mean I want to start listening to you.' He grinned, blushing. Appalled at herself, she knew it was hopeless with them – he was sweet and dear but nothing would stop him going to meetings the rest of his life and she could not bear to be good any more, she wanted glory.

She drew his head to her lips, kissing his brow like a benediction. In death's shadow, she thought, we part in love. He let her hand slide out of his fingers and moved to the door where he turned to look back at her one last time; romantic! She stood in their doorway watching him as he waited in the corridor for the elevator. When its door clanked open she raised a hand and wiggled her fingers, giving him her smile and her irony. 'Proud of you, soldier!' He threw her a kiss and backed into the elevator. Would he die? She threw herself on to their bed, dry-eyed, wondering who in the world she was as she filled up with love for this noble man.

He might be gone a year. Maybe two. No one knew. She registered at Hunter as a graduate student in art history. It was perfect; her good husband off to the War in the best imaginable cause, and she in New York and not some God-forsaken army camp, taking courses with Profes-sor Oscar Kalkofsky.

The War continued its unrelenting grip on time; the 'Duration' calcified most decisions, nothing long-term could be started until peace came, in probably five or six years it was thought now. Frustration was mitigated by the solace of having a ready excuse for everything undone or put off – like confronting Sam with a divorce when he was off fighting in Germany and might well be sent to the Pacific for the assault on Japan.

But suddenly the Bomb settled that and everyone was coming home. Where would she find the strength to tell Sam that she could not be with him any more? She must find a job, an independence from which to address him. She walked endlessly in Manhattan, tensed, half-angry, half-afraid, trying to conjure up a possible career for herself, and finally one day went to see Professor Kalkofsky to talk not about art but about her life.

Months earlier, tired of walking, she had stopped by the Argosy store on lower 5th Avenue to get off her feet and look for something new to read, and was talking to Peter Berger, the owner's son and Sam's immediate boss, when the Professor came in. Almost immediately his quiet self-mocking smile and wry fatalism drew her in, an affectation of weariness so patently flirtatious that it amused her. And his gaze kept flicking to her calves, her best feature.

A gentle, platinum-haired giant, in his office one afternoon he sat with European academic propriety, both enormous shoes set on the floor, his pipe smouldering in his right hand whose two missing fingers, broken off by a Nazi torturer, spoke to her of a reality the Atlantic Ocean had sterilised before it reached America. She was sure he was not only taken with her but that he had no thought of a future for any relationship; his witty eyes and unsmiling mouth, some adamance in his unspoken demand on her, and his quiet speech that day — it all seemed to be solemnly taking charge of her body. Despite his bulk and manner there was something womanly about him; she thought that unlike most men he seemed unafraid of sex.

'Is not very complicated, Mrs Fink.' She liked his not using her first name yet and hoped, if they made love, he would continue calling her Mrs Fink in bed. 'After war like this, will be necessary to combine two contradictory drives. First, how to glamorise, as you say, cooperative modes in new society; at same time, incorporate pleasure-ethic which certainly must sweep world after so much deprivation. That means following; to take what is offered, ask for it if it is not offered, regret nothing. The regret element is main thing; once you accept that you have chosen to be as you are, incredible as that seems, then regret is not possible. We have been slaves to this war and to Fascism. If Communism is brought to Poland and Europe, will never last long in countries of the

Renaissance. So now we are free, the slavery is finished, or will soon be. We are going to have to learn how to select self, and so to be free.'

She had read existentialist philosophy but had never been, so to speak, seduced by it, armoured as she was with the decade of Puritanical Marxism that followed the disgraced Jazz Age of her father. But there was more to her fascination; Europeans liked talking about submerged connecting themes rather than mere disjointed events, and she loved this, thinking she might figure herself out if she could only generalise with precision. But it never quite happened. As though she had known him a long time — which in a way she had — she began telling about her life. 'I realise I don't have any kind of standard look, but . . .' He did not interrupt with a reassuring false compliment, and this meant he accepted her exactly as she was. This thrilled her with sudden possibilities. '. . . But I . . . I forgot what I was starting to say.' She laughed, her head full of lights, admitting a hunger for something to happen between them beyond speech.

'I think what you are saying is you don't feel you have ever really made a choice in life.'

Of course! How could he possibly have known that? She was drifting with no real goal. . . . She felt her hair, suddenly believing it must be tangled.

And he said, 'I know it because I see how much expectation there is in you.' Yes, that was it! 'Almost any suffering is tolerable provided you have chosen it. I was in London when they attacked Poland, but I knew I must go back and I also knew the danger if I did. When he broke my fingers I understood why the Church was so strong – was built by men who had chosen to suffer for it. My pain was also chosen and that dimension of choice, you see, made it significant, was not wasted, not nothing.'

Then he simply reached out over the arm of his chair and gripped her hand and drew her to him and meditatively kissed her lips, closing his eyes as though she symbolised something for him and his wise European suffering. She immediately knew what the years-long aching in her really was – simply that she had never truly chosen Sam, he had kind of happened to her because – yes, because she had never thought of herself like this, as a woman of value choosing to grant herself. He slipped his hand into her clothing and even the cynicism of his cool expertise pleased her with its brazen consciousness.

She looked down at him kneeling on the floor

with his face buried between her thighs. 'I love knowing what I'm doing, don't you?' she said, and laughed.

His face was broad and very white, its bones thick and strong. He looked up at her and, making a wry mouth, said, 'The post-War era begins.' But he kept it wry, just this side of laughter.

· III ·

After Sam's return in September, whole guilty months passed before she could dare to tell him that she could no longer bear it with him. It came about by accident.

Bringing it up had been difficult because he behaved once again as though they had never had a problem; and it didn't help that somewhere in him he was taking a substantial amount of credit for destroying Fascism. His prophetic Marxism had proved itself in Russia's new post-War power and Fascism's extinction and set him consciously as a participant in history, nobly at that. A new note, something close to arrogance, a quality she had formerly wished for him, irritated her now that their spirits had parted. But what set her off was his implying one evening that he had forced himself on a German farm woman who had given him shelter in a rainstorm one night.

She grinned, fascinated. 'Tell me about it; was she married?'

'Oh sure; the husband was gone, she thought he'd been captured or killed at Stalingrad.'

'How old was she, young?'

'About thirty, thirty-two.'

'Good-looking?'

'Well, kind of heavy.' In his gruff laugh she saw that he had probably decided not to be obsequious with her any more. His lovemaking since his return had been markedly overbearing but no less inept than before; he was better at handling her body but her feelings seemed to have no space in his mind.

'And what happened? Tell me.'

'Well, Bavaria . . . we were stuck in this half-bombed out town hall with the wind blowing through the windows, and I had a cold that was killing me. Coming into town I'd noticed this house half a mile or so off down the road, and it'd looked tight and had smoke coming out of the chimney. So I went over. She gave me some soup. She was too stupid to hide the Nazi flag hanging over her husband's picture. And it got late and I . . .' He pursed his lips cutely, stretched out his legs, and clasped his hands behind his head. 'You really want to hear this?'

'Come on, dear, you know you want to tell it.'

'Okay. I said I wanted to spend the night and she showed me to this tiny cold room near the kitchen. And I said, "Look, you Nazi bitch, I am sleeping in the best bed in this house. . . ." '

She laughed excitedly. 'That's wonderful. And what did she do?'

'Well, she let me have her and her husband's bedroom.' He left it at that.

She sensed the gap, and grinned broadly. 'And? Come on, what happened?' He was blushing, but pridefully. 'Was she hot stuff or what? Come on! She grab for you?'

'Not at all. She was a real Nazi.'

'You mean you raped her?'

'I don't know if you'd call it rape,' he said, clearly hoping she would.

'Well, did she want to or not?'

'What's the difference? It wasn't all that bad.'

'And how long'd you stay with her?'

'Just two nights, till we pulled out.'

'And was she anti-Nazi by then?' She grinned at him.

'I didn't ask.'

His pride in it filled her with wonder, and release. 'And did she have blonde braids and a dirndl?'

'Not a dirndl.'

'But blonde braids.'

'As a matter of fact, yes.'

'And big breasts?'

'Well, it was Bavaria,' he said before he could catch himself, and they both burst out laughing. She walked to his chair and bent over and kissed his tonsure. He looked up at her with love and pride in his achievement.

'I'm leaving you, Sam,' she said, a touch of humour still in her voice. Suddenly, she no longer had to reach down to sustain him. He would be all right.

After his disbelief, his shock and anger, she said, 'You'll be fine, dear.' She made a Martini and crossed her legs under her on the couch as though for a nice chat.

'But where will you go?' Truly, it was as though with a face like hers he was her only possible harbour in the world.

The insult was even worse because he was unaware of it, and she instantly raged against the time she had wasted with him. She had developed a way of chuckling softly when hurt, tucking in her chin and looking up at her opponent with raised eyebrows and then unwinding her ironies as off a spool of wire.

'Well, now that you mention it, it would hardly matter where I went since to all intents and purposes I am nowhere now.' She waited an instant. 'Don't you think so, Sam?'

·IV·

In its seedy Parisian ornateness the Crosby Hotel on 71st off Broadway was still fairly decent then, at the end of the War, and it was wonderful to have a room with nothing in it of her own. How great to have no future! Free again. It reminded her a little of the Voltaire on the Quai in '39 with her father in the next room tapping on the wall to wake her for breakfast. She dared to call Lionel Mayer – 'I wondered if you needed any typing done,' bantering with him on the phone like a teenager, dangling herself before him and taking it all back when pressed; clearly, with no war to direct his life he was as lost as she was, a deeply unhappy young man posing as a *paterfamilias*, and soon he was standing with his crotch pressed against her head as she sat typing an article he had written for Colliers on his Philippines experiences. But she had no illusions, or the merest inevitable ones that only lasted while he was in her, and when she was alone her emptiness ached and she felt fear for herself, passing thirty now with no one at all.

Herman came one afternoon to see how she lived. He had lost some weight. 'No more trains, I fly now. I'm buying in Chicago. You can pick up half the city for beans.' He sat glancing out disapprovingly at upper Broadway. 'This is a dump, sister, you picked a real good dump to waste your life in. What was wrong with Sam, too intellectual? I thought you liked intellectuals. Why don't you come in with me, we form a company, the cities are full of great buys, we can put down ten, fifteen per cent and own a building, get mortgages to fix it up, raise the rents as high as you want, and walk away with fifty per cent on your money.'

'And what happens to the people living in those buildings?'

'They start paying a decent rent or go where they can afford. It's economics, Janice, the country is off welfare, we're moving into the biggest boom there ever was, 1920s all over again, get on board and get out of this dump.' He had eyeglasses now, when he remembered to wear them. He put them on to show her. 'I'm turning thirty-six, baby, but I feel terrific. How about you?'

'I expect to feel happy but I'm not terrific yet. But you can't have my money to throw people out on the street. Sorry, dear.' She wanted to change her stockings, still wore silk despite the new nylons which felt clammy to her. Starting to open a drawer in the old dresser the knob came off in her hand.

'How can you live in this dump, everything falling apart?'

'I like everything falling apart, it's less competition for when I start falling apart.'

'By the way, you never found those ashes, did you.'

'What brings that up?'

'I don't know, I was just reminded because it was his birthday last August.' He scratched his heavy leg and glanced again out the window. 'He'd have given you the same advice. People with heads are going to be millionaires in the next five years. Real estate in New York is undervalued, and there's thousands walking around looking for decent apartments. I need somebody with me I can trust. By the way, what do you do all day? I mean it, you have a funny look to me, Janice. You look like your mind is not concentrated any more. Am I wrong?'

She rolled a stocking up her leg, careful to keep the seam straight. 'I don't want my mind concentrated, I want it receptive to what's around me. Does that seem odd or dishonourable? I'm trying to find out what I have to do to live like a person. I read books, I read philosophical novels like Camus, and I read dead poets like Emily Dickinson, and I also . . .'

'It doesn't look to me like you have any friends, do you?'

'Why? Do friends leave traces? Maybe I'm not ready to have friends. Maybe I'm not fully born yet. Hindus believe that, you know – they think we go on being born and reborn right through life, or something like that. Life is very painful to me, Herman.'

Tears had flowed into her eyes. This ridiculous person was her brother, the last person in the world she would think of confiding in, yet she trusted him more than anyone she had known, as ludicrous and overweight as he still was. She sat on the bed and saw him by the slanting grey light through the dirty window, a young blob full of plans and greed's happiness.

'I love this city,' she said, with no special point

in mind. 'I know there are ways to be happy in it but I haven't found any. But I know they're there.' She went to the other front window and parted the dusty lace curtain and looked down at Broadway. She could smell the soot on the window. A light drizzle had begun to fall.

'I'm buying a new Cadillac.'

'Aren't they awfully big? How can you drive them?'

'Like silk. You float. They're fantastic. We're trying to have a baby again, I don't want a car that joggles her belly.'

'Are you really as confident as you seem?'

'Absolutely. Come with me.'

'I don't think I want to be that rich.'

'I think you're still communistic.'

'I guess so. There's something wrong, living for money. I don't want to start.'

'At least get out of those bonds and get into the market. You're literally losing money every hour.'

'Am I? Well, I don't feel it so the hell with it.'

He heaved up on to his feet and buttoned his blue jacket, pulled his tie down and picked his topcoat off the back of a chair. 'I will never understand you, Janice.'

'That makes two of us, Herman.'

'What are you going to do the rest of the day? I mean just as an instance.'

'An instance of what?'

'Of what you do with your days.'

'They play old movies on 72nd Street, I may go there. There's a Garbo, I think.'

'In the middle of a working day.'

'I love being in the movies when it's drizzling out.'

'You want to come home with me for dinner?'

'No, dear. It might jiggle her belly.' She laughed and quickly kissed him to take the sting out of that remark, which she had been as unprepared for as he. But in truth she did not want children, ever.

'What do you want out of life, do you know?'

'Of course I know.'

'What?'

'A good time.'

He shook his head, baffled. 'Don't get in trouble,' he said as he left.

·V·

S he adored Garbo, anything she played, could sit through two showings of even the most wooden of her films, they released her irony. She loved to be set afloat and pushed out to sea by these creakingly factitious Graustarkian tales and their hilarious swan-shaped bathtubs and eagle-head taps, their dripping Baroque doors and windows and drapes. Nowadays their glorious vileness of taste cheered her to the point of levitation, of hysteria, cut her free of all her education, rejoined her with her country. It made her want to stand on a roof and scream happily at the stars when the actress emerged from a noble white Rolls without ever catching a heel on a filmy long dress. Her languorous posing on *chaises longues*, the mile-long world weariness of her moody jousts with her leading men and finally the permission she gave her ceramic eyelids pleasurably to close at Barrymore's long-

delayed kiss, all this was a fall away from the dull
flat platforms of the world. And of course
Garbo's cheekbones and the fabulous reflective-
ness of her perfect white skin, the carved planes
of interest in her face, were proof of God's glory
more convincing than Reims. Janice could lie on
her hotel bed facing the ceiling and hardly blink
for an hour as the Garbo face hung over her eyes.
She could stand before her dressing-table mirrors
which cut her off at the neck and find her body
surprisingly ready and alive with a certain flow,
especially from a side view which emphasised her
good thighs.

·VI·

The creaky elevator door opened one afternoon and she saw standing before it a
handsome man in his forties – or possibly his
early fifties, with a walking stick in one hand and
a briefcase in the other. With an oddly straight-
backed walk he entered the elevator and Janice
only realised he was blind when he stopped
hardly six inches from her and then turned
himself to face the door by lifting his feet instead
of simply swivelling about. There was a shaving
cut on his chin.

'Going down, aren't we?'

'Yes, down.' She felt a quickened surge in her
chest. A freedom close by, liberation as for one
instant he stared sightless into her face.

At the lobby he walked straight out and across
the tiled floor to the glass doors to the street. She
hung on behind him and pushed the doors open
for him. 'May I help you?'

'Thanks, yes, thanks very much.'

He walked into the street and turned directly right toward Broadway and she came up alongside him. 'Do you go to the subway? I mean that's where I'm going if you'd like me to stay with you.'

'Oh, that'd be fine, yes. Thank you, although I can make it myself.'

'But as long as I'm going, too.'

She walked beside him, he kept a surprisingly good pace. What life in his fluttering eyelids! It was like walking with a sighted man but the freedom she felt alongside him was bringing tears of relief and gratitude to her eyes. She found herself pouring all her feeling into her voice which suddenly flew out of her mouth with the joyful innocence of a young girl's.

His voice had a dry flatness as though not often used. 'Have you lived in the hotel long?'

'Since March. Since my divorce,' she added without a qualm. 'And you?'

'Oh, I've been there for five years now. The walls on the twelfth floor are just about sound-proof, you know.'

'You play an instrument?'

'The piano. I'm with Decca, in the classical division, I listen to a lot of recordings at home.'

'That's very interesting.' She felt his pleasure in this nice conversation without tension, she could sense his gratitude to her as they walked. He was lonely. People probably avoided him or were too formal or something. She celebrated her instinct for a moment, had never felt more sure of herself, more free.

At the top of the subway steps she took his arm with a light grasp as though he were a bird she might scare off. He did not resist and at the turnstile insisted on paying her fare out of a handful of nickels he had ready. She had no idea where he was going or where she could pretend to be going.

'How do you know where to get off?'

'I count the stops.'

'Oh, of course, how stupid.'

'I go to 57th.'

'That's where I'm going.'

'You work around there?'

'Actually, I'm kind of still settling in. But I'm on the lookout for something.'

'Well, you shouldn't have a problem, you seem very young.'

'Actually, I wasn't really going anywhere, I just wanted to help you.'

'Really?'

'Yes.'

'What's your name?'

'Janice Sessions. What's yours?'

'Charles Buckman.'

She wanted to ask if he was married but clearly he couldn't be, must not be, something about him was deeply organised and not hostage to anything or anyone.

Out on the street he halted at the curb facing uptown. 'I go to the Athletic Club on 59th.'

'May I walk with you?'

'Certainly. I work out for an hour before the office.'

'You look very fit.'

'You should do it. Although I think you're fit, too.'

'How can you tell?'

'The way you put your feet down.'

'Really!'

'Oh yes, that tells a lot. Let me have your hand.'

She quickly put her left hand in his right. He pressed her palm with his index and middle fingers and let her hand go. 'You're in pretty good shape but it would be a good thing to swim, your wind isn't very great.'

She felt thrilled, embraced by the sweep of his

uncanny knowledge of her. 'Maybe I will.' She hated exercise but vowed to begin as soon as she could. Under the grey canopy of the Athletic Club he slowed to a halt and faced her and for the first time she could look for more than an instant past his flickering lids directly into his brown eyes. She felt she would choke with amazed gratitude, for he was smiling slightly as though pleased to be seen looking so intimately at her in this very public place. She felt herself standing more erectly than she ever had since she was born.

'I'm in 1214 if you'd like to come up for a drink.'

'I'd love it.' She laughed at her instantaneous acceptance. 'I must tell you,' she said, and heard herself with a terror of embarrassment but resolved not to quail before the need exploding in herself, 'you've made me incredibly happy.'

'Happy? Why?'

He was beginning to blush. It amazed her that embarrassment could penetrate his nearly immobile face.

'I don't know why. You just have. I feel you know me better than anyone ever has. I'm sorry I'm being so silly.'

'No-no. Please, be sure to come tonight.'

'Oh, I will.'

She felt she could stretch up and kiss his lips and that he wouldn't mind because she was beautiful. Or her hand was.

'You can turn off the light, if you like.'

'I don't know. Maybe I'd rather leave it on.'

He slipped out of his shorts and felt for the bed with his shin and lay down beside her as she stared into his sightless face. His hand discovered her good happy body. It was pure touch, pure truth beyond speech. Everything she was was moving through his hand like water unfrozen. She was free of her whole life and kissed him hard and tenderly, praying that there be a god who would keep her from error with him, and moved his hands where she wished them to be, mastering him and enslaving herself to his slightest movements.

In a respite he ran his fingers over her face and she held her breath hearing his breaths suspending as he felt the curve of her nose, her long upper lip and forehead, lightly pressed her cheekbones – discovering, she was sure, that they lacked distinction and were buried in a rounded yet tightened face.

'I am not beautiful,' she asked more than stated.

'You are, where it matters to me.'

'Can you picture me?'

'Very well, yes.'

'Is it really all right?'

'What earthly difference can it possibly make to me?' He rolled over on top of her placing his mouth on hers, then moving over her face read it with his lips. His pleasure poured into her again.

'I will die here, my heart will stop right here under you because I don't need any more than this and I can't bear it.'

'I like your lisp.'

'Do you? It doesn't sound childish?'

'It does, that's why I like it. What colour is your hair?'

'Can you imagine colours?'

'I think I can imagine black, is it black?'

'No, it's kind of chestnut, slightly reddish chestnut and very straight. It falls almost to my shoulders. My head is large and my mouth is on the large side too and slightly prognathous. But I walk nicely, maybe beautifully if you ask some people, I love to walk in a sexy way.'

'Your ass is wonderfully shaped.'

'Yes, I forgot to mention that.'

'It thrilled me to hold it.'

'I'm glad.' Then she added, 'I'm really dumb-foundedly glad.'

'And how do I look to you?'

'I think you're a splendidly handsome man. You have darkish skin and brown hair parted on the left, and a nicely shaped strong chin. Your face is kind of rectangular I guess, kind of reassuring and silent. You are about three or four inches taller than me and your body is slim but not skinny. I think you are spectacular-looking.'

He chuckled. She held his penis. 'And this is perfection.' He laughed and kissed her lightly. Then quietly he fell asleep. She lay beside him not daring to stir and wake him to life and its dangers again.

In the seventies, living in the Village, she read in the papers that the Crosby Hotel was being demolished for a new apartment house. She was working as a volunteer now for a civil rights organisation monitoring violations everywhere, both East and West, and decided to take an extra hour after lunch and to go uptown to see the old hotel once more before it vanished. She was into her sixties now, and Charles had died in his sleep a little more than a year earlier. She came out of the subway and walked down the side street and found that the top floor, the twelfth, was already gone. She leaned against a building up the street from the hotel and watched the men prising apart the brick walls with surprising ease. So it was more or less only gravity that held buildings up! She could see inside rooms, the different colours people had painted the walls, what care had been taken to select the right shade! With each falling piece of masonry billowing bursts of dust rushed upwards into the air. Each generation takes part of the city away, like ants tugging twigs. Soon they would be reaching her old room. An empty amazement crept over her. Out of sixty-one years of life she had had fourteen good ones. Not bad.

She thought of the dozens of recitals and concerts, the dinners in restaurants, the utterness of Charles's love and reliance on her who had become his eyes. In a way he had turned her inside out so that she looked out at the world instead of holding her breath for the world to look at her and disapprove. She walked up closer to the front doors of the hotel and stood there across the street, catching the haunted earth-cold smell of a dying building, trying to recapture that first time she had walked out with him into the street and then down to the subway, the last day of her homeliness. She had bought a new perfume and it floated up to her through the dusty air and pleased her.

She turned back to Broadway and strolled past the fruit stands and the debris of collisions lying on the curbs, the broken pizza crusts of the city's eaters in the streets, fruit peels and cores, a lost boot and a rotted tie, a woman sitting on the sidewalk combing her hair, the black boys ranting after a basketball, the implosion of causes and purposes she had once known and could no longer find the strength to call back from the quickly disappearing past. And Charles arm in arm with her here, walking imperturbably through it all with his hat flat straight on his head and his crimson muffler around his throat and whistling softly but so strongly the mighty main theme of *Harold In Italy*. Oh Death, oh Death, she said almost aloud, waiting on the corner for the light to change, and wondering at her fortune at having lived into beauty.

Also by Arthur Miller
and available from Methuen

Plays: One

All My Sons, Death of a Salesman,
The Crucible, A Memory of Two Mondays,
A View from the Bridge

This first volume of Arthur Miller's Collected Plays contains four of the most famous stage-plays from the whole of the American theatre, all written within a ten-year period which began with Miller's first Broadway hit.

'With the production of *All My Sons*,' wrote Brooks Atkinson of the *New York Times* in 1947, 'the theatre has acquired a genuine new talent. Arthur Miller . . . has written an honest, forceful drama about a group of people caught up in a monstrous swindle that has caused the death of twenty-one American pilots.'

'A great play of our day,' wrote the *New York Herald Tribune*'s Howard Barnes in 1949. '*Death of a Salesman* has majesty, sweep and shattering dramatic impact . . . The story of Willy Loman, who lived for a strange dream and tried to have it realised by a worthless son, while destroying the boy, has its roots deep in the complex structure of contemporary existence.'

Reviewing *The Crucible* in 1953 — seen then as a parable of McCarthyism — Brooks Atkinson wrote in the *New York Times*: 'Riffling back the pages of American history Miller has written the drama of the witch trials and the hangings in Salem in 1692. Neither Mr Miller nor his audiences are unaware of certain similarities between the perversions of justice then and today.' But Miller himself sees the play as examining 'the conflict between a man's raw deed and his conception of himself'.

'*A View from the Bridge*' concerns present-day life in a colony of Italian-American longshoremen on the Brooklyn waterfront,' wrote John Chapman of the *New York Daily News* in 1955. 'It is a tragedy in classic form, and I think it is a modern classic . . .

Arthur Miller has come a long way in our theatre and he will go much farther.'

Also included are *A Memory of Two Mondays*, a one-act play about life in a motor parts warehouse, originally written to accompany *A View from the Bridge*, and an extensive introduction by the author.

Plays: Two

The Misfits, After the Fall,
Incident at Vichy, The Price,
The Creation of the World and Other Business,
Playing for Time

This second volume of Arthur Miller's Collected Plays contains
two pieces associated with his then wife, Marilyn Monroe, two
pieces on aspects of the Second World War, a dramatisation of
the Adam and Eve story, and a domestic piece with a strong vein
of autobiography.

Miller himself describes his screenplay for *The Misfits* – filmed in
1961 by John Huston with Monroe, Montgomery Clift and
Clark Gable – as a 'gift' for Marilyn, 'a story of three men who
cannot locate a home on earth for themselves, and, for
something to do, capture wild horses to be butchered for canned
dog food; and a woman as homeless as they, but whose intact
sense of life's sacredness suggests a meaning for existence.'

Maggie in *After the Fall* (1964) was, to Miller's surprise, reduced
to 'a portrait, purely and simply, of Marilyn . . . The play was
about how we – nations and individuals – destroy ourselves by
denying that this is precisely what we are doing.'

The root of *Incident at Vichy* (1964), set in Nazi-occupied France,
lies in the story of 'a Jewish analyst picked up with false papers
and saved by a man he had never seen before'.

In *The Price* (1968) 'two brothers meet again after an angry
break-up many years before; the time has come to divide the
family's possessions after the father's death. Grown men now,
they think they have achieved the indifference to the betrayals of
the past that maturity confers. But it all comes back . . .'

Similarly, '*The Creation of the World and Other Business* (1972), reconsidering Genesis, was essentially the fratricidal enigma, but seen now as a given of man's nature.'

Playing for Time, a screenplay filmed in 1980 with Vanessa Redgrave, returns to the Second World War with the story of a women's orchestra formed from Auschwitz inmates and of two of the women's attempts at survival in such circumstances.

The volume carries a brief introduction by the author.

Plays: Three

The American Clock, The Archbishop's Ceiling, Two-Way Mirror

In *The American Clock*, Miller offers a cross-section of American society during the Great Depression and harks back to those qualities and values which helped America to survive. It is also a warning from Miller to his fellow Americans: 'There's never been a country that hasn't had a clock running on it,' says one of his characters, 'so I keep asking myself – how long?'

Set in an Eastern European capital, in a room which is probably bugged, *The Archbishop's Ceiling* was written in 1977, in the aftermath of Watergate, and is a powerful elegy for the fate of the individual in an age when power is the sole remaining ideology of both East and West. It deals with the question of how 'real' human behaviour can be under the ubiquitous threat of surveillance, where everyone is turned into performers.

Two-Way Mirror consists of two short plays: *Elegy for a Lady* and *Some Kind of Love Story*. In the first play, an ageing, married businessman comes into a classy boutique searching for a present for a dying lover who has cut off all contact with him. It has been described by the author as 'a play of shadows under the tree of death'. *Some Kind of Love Story* is a deeply ironic thriller in which an innocent man has been jailed for murder and the police and the judiciary appear to have played an active role in this miscarriage of justice.

The volume carries a brief introduction by the author.

Plays: Four

*The Golden Years, The Man Who Had All The Luck,
I Can't Remember Anything, Clara*

The Golden Years is a historical tragedy about Montezuma's
destruction at the hands of Cortez. Unable to convert the Aztecs,
Cortez assumes the role of barbarian, ravager of a civilisation,
while Montezuma convinces himself that the strange white
creatures who came out of the ocean are fated both to be his
masters and to apotheosise him to godhead. 'A contemplation of
history, a character study, a drama of conflicting myths and
values, it stands out from Miller's other plays of the 1930s,' writes
Christopher Bigsby, 'in its language and in its subtlety of thought
and action.'

The Man Who Had All The Luck is a fable about human freedom
and individual responsibility, whose hero, David Beeves, acts out
an ironic reversal of Job's plight. Plagued by the contrast
between his own success and the failures of those around him, he
tries to make sense of his good fortune. 'A fascinating revelation,'
wrote Michael Coveney in the *Observer*, 'a Mid-West idyll of
fatalistic optimism written as the young Miller wavered between
fiction and the stage.'

I Can't Remember Anything and *Clara* were first produced in
London in 1988 as a double bill, *Danger: Memory! I Can't
Remember Anything* is a funny and touching two-hander about
two elderly people, Leo and Leonora, and Leonora's resistance to
the past, its pain and irony. *Clara* is a starker play in the form of a
police interrogation of Kroll, the father of a woman who has
been brutally murdered. Kroll, also initially resistant to the past,
finally acknowledges the good action which set off his daughter's
murder. John Peter wrote in the *Sunday Times:* 'Their psychological penetration is sharp, supple and vigorous. Each play unfolds
into the past, into the recesses of people's minds.'

The volume carries an introduction by the author and an afterword by Christopher Bigsby.

Plays: Five

The Last Yankee, The Ride Down Mount Morgan,
Almost Everybody Wins

'*The Last Yankee*' reasserts Miller's unquestionable dominace of American drama,' wrote John Peter in the *Sunday Times*. 'No other American playwright has had his range of judgement with his warm and forgiving sense of humour and his ability to inhabit completely, like Shakespeare or Ibsen, every character he creates . . . Miller writes with a sense of pain and laughter, with an understanding of the heart's endless struggle with the mind, which is characteristic of a writer on an unending journey of discovery.'

'Arthur Miller has written a fine and moving play,' wrote Michael Billington in the *Guardian*. 'What makes this a first-rate play is that Miller allows the ideas to grow from the characters . . . this is a political play with strong human texture.'

About *The Ride Down Mount Morgan*, John Peter wrote, again in the *Sunday Times:* 'Searching, scorching, harsh but compassionate . . . This is the funniest play he has written. But it is an acid laughter, too, a laughter of bitter wisdom; and under the comic trimmings a serious moral and psychological argument is going on.' Further, Andrew St George wrote in the *Financial Times*: 'Comedy if one thinks, tragedy if one feels.'

This volume also contains *Almost Everybody Wins*, the original version of the screenplay Arthur Miller wrote for Karel Reisz's film *Everybody Wins* (1990), and an introduction by the author.

Broken Glass

Brooklyn, 1939: Sylvia Gellburg is stricken by a mysterious paralysis in her legs for which the doctor can find no cause. He soon realises that she is obsessed by the devastating news from Germany, where government thugs have begun smashing Jewish stores. But this event is coiled around what he learns is her strange relationship with her husband Phillip. When the two seemingly unrelated situations concatenate, a tragic flare of light opens on the age. *Broken Glass* received its British première at the Royal National Theatre in August 1994.

'His strongest play for many years, a gripping and at times powerfully affecting drama. As almost always in his work, it balances private lives with public morality,' wrote Charles Spencer in the *Daily Telegraph*. 'It is also an amazingly full-blooded piece, bursting with pain and passion.'

'For a long time after you leave the theatre, Arthur Miller's new play echoes and resonates in your mind,' wrote John Peter in the *Sunday Times*. 'This grand, harrowing play, deeply compassionate and darkly humorous, is one of the great creations of the American theatre.'

And Michael Billington wrote in the *Guardian*: 'A wise, humane and moving play'.

I Don't Need You Any More

Arthur Miller's stories are as finely constructed and as expressive as any of his work for the theatre. *I Don't Need You Any More* is a collection of nine stories and includes the original version of *The Misfits*, which later became the classic, celebrated film.

Ranging in theme from the title story's bold and impressionistic evocation of a few late summer days in a young boy's life to the tale of an American Jew's poignant discovery in a tiny Italian mountain town, and to the contradictory anxieties that accompany celebrity, some of these tales are novelistic in their complexity, others are anecdotal – taken together they add to Miller's established reputation as one of the greatest writers of our times.

Timebends

'This book could hardly have failed. Arthur Miller has been a dominant figure in the American theatre for over forty years, author of *Death of a Salesman* and *View from the Bridge*. Meanwhile his public, political career has been very active. And he was married to Marilyn Monroe. So, the historical interest of *Timebends* comes as no surprise; but its power and quality are a revelation . . . Arthur Miller's achievement in this book is to fuse the rhetorical power of his drama with the steely integrity of his life. The result is something pretty close to a masterpiece'

Sean French

'The personality revealed by this fine autobiography is wholly admirable. Miller did more than fracture the American dream and interpret the American nightmare: he dared to enter the fire that surrounded the most potent sexual myth of the century'

Anthony Burgess

'A book and a half. Arthur Miller is that very rare bird: a truly independent man. His autobiography is a beautifully structured narrative: tough, very moving, a political testimony of considerable force'

Harold Pinter

'The most powerful autobiography by a living author I have ever come across'

Sheridan Morley

Selection from the works of **Arthur Miller** available from Methuen

ISBN	TITLE	PRICE
☐ 0 413 15810 1	Plays: 1	£9.99
☐ 0 413 15820 9	Plays: 2	£9.99
☐ 0 413 63500 7	Plays: 3	£9.99
☐ 0 413 68010 X	Plays: 4	£9.99
☐ 0 413 69830 0	Plays: 5	£9.99
☐ 0 413 68190 4	Broken Glass	£6.99
☐ 0 413 70980 9	The Crucible (screenplay)	£6.99
☐ 0 413 74670 4	Plain Girl	£6.99
☐ 0 413 74660 7	I Don't Need You Any More	£7.99
☐ 0 413 563804	'Salesman' in Beijing	£9.99
☐ 0 413 66920 3	The Theatre Essays of Arthur Miller	£9.99
☐ 0 413 77340 X	Timebends	£9.99

• All Methuen books are available through mail order or from your local bookshop.
Please send cheque/eurocheque/postal order (sterling only) Access, Visa, Mastercard, Diners
Card, Switch or Amex.

☐☐☐☐☐☐☐☐☐☐☐☐☐☐☐☐

Expiry Date: _____ Signature: _____

UK customers please allow £1 for the first book and 50p thereafter up to a maximum of
£3 for post and packing.
Overseas customers please allow £1.50 for the first book and 75p thereafter up to a
maximum of £5 for post and packing.
ALL ORDERS TO:
Methuen Books, Books by Post, TBS Limited, The Book Service, Colchester Road,
Frating Green, Colchester, Essex CO7 7DW.

NAME: _____

ADDRESS: _____

_____

_____

Please allow 28 days for delivery. Please tick box if you do not
wish to receive any additional information   ☐

Prices and availability subject to change without notice.